A Beginner's Compass to Navigating

Cyber Security

Copyright © 2024 by Jignesh Tank

First Edition: 2024

This book is a work of non-fiction. While the author has utilised the best efforts in preparing this book, the information contained herein is provided "as is" and without specific warranties of any kind or type and accepts no liabilities for any direct or indirect damages resulting from its use.

Preface

The digital world is rapidly expanding and with it, the challenges and threats we face online. As someone who has spent over a decade in the field of cybersecurity, I've seen first-hand how crucial it is to protect ourselves in this developing vista. My motivation for writing this book stems from a deep concern for the younger generation those who are most active on social media and online platforms. You stand at the threshold of this digital age and it is now upon you to understand and know what these nuances of cybersecurity mean not for safeguarding alone but to be the guardians of your future.

While helping others, one question has been echoing from the bottoms of the hearts of the young souls: "How do I get into Cybersecurity?" Well, this book is an attempt to tell you just that and quench your curious mind as to how this fascinating discipline works.

The book is well thought through and follows the adolescent from about 13 to 25 years of age very enthused about cybersecurity.

So, if you already fiddle with a computer, are intrigued by hacking or just wonder how the internet works, this book is for you. My aim is to give you a good grounding in cybersecurity and introduce you to a broad range of topics within this field while giving you ideas about where this might take you in your career.

It goes from defining what it is to the multiple paths one might take to achieve a successful career. Writing this book was no mean task. Being an amateur writer, I could not get myself to be disciplined enough or even write in a manner that would make sense to you, the real reader. This project is accomplished with determination, unrelenting drive and a well-nurtured passion with this subject. I hope that it comes out to be yet another asset for you. Allow me to take a moment to thank all those who supported me in this work. Varsha, my wife who was a constant encouragement; parents, who instilled in me the importance of education; and friends, who would stand by me through this entire process.

Finally, a personal observation on my journey, I have run into several youth who are really confused about how to get into the world of cybersecurity. Most of them turned towards me to seek advice and insight from me to mentor and coach them. This book is for those amongst the readership who want to learn, have the passion and that too beyond words but probably would need some direction. I'm sure this deep dives you into the world of cybersecurity while at the same time enflaming your desire to protect our future in the digital world.

Thank you, I appreciate you having been with me through the journey. I really look forward to seeing where it takes you.

Sincerely,
Jignesh Tank

Table of Contents

Chapter 1: The Cyber World Unleashed

Hi there, budding Cyber Explorers! Ever wondered what's going on behind that box with the glowing lights when you're chatting with your friends, laughing at funny cat videos or playing the latest online game? Maybe you overheard bigger kids, even adults, talk about "hackers" and "viruses" and wondered what that meant? Well, get set to take a journey through an amazing, sometimes scary but always exciting world of cybersecurity!

What's Cybersecurity Anyway?

Consider for a moment that the Internet is like a huge and complex cityscape, packed with towering skyscrapers which represent the many millions of websites out there like YouTube, Instagram and so on. There are bustling markets within this cityscape, filled with commerce, and a large online emporium such as Amazon. The most important fact is that beneath the surface, below the streets and in the dark of night, there runs the underworld of tunnels, the dark web where hidden people engage in hurtful and illegal actions to perform their sinister deals and transactions. Moreover, throughout this digital realm, there exist treasure chests holding your personal information: your name, your home address and your posted photos. The metaphor can also run deeper just as every cityscape needs protection against dangers and threats, so does the Internet need protection and the absolutely vital field of cybersecurity brings it this protection.

Cybersecurity can be definitely considered, without any hesitation as the strong and mighty army guarding the digital city from a host of different and destructive threats. Therefore, bright engineers with fine skills and knowledge together with sly and stealthy code-breaking ninjas that are good at the arts of infiltration and deception form excellent inclusions on the list of defenders for the city. This shining legion will be patrolling up and down every street incessantly with their checks held high and visible, ever so keenly watching every network, pursuing with extra care any stray event which may take place and last but not least, building an unbreakable wall with a state-of-the-art alarm system by ingeniously crafting solid and effective security software. Followed by the good news, you're just about to step in likely their most elite rank!

Introducing the Cyber Avengers

You might wonder who these Cyber Avengers are. In reality, they comprise the good guys, fighting a constant battle against these cyber villains, those no-good hackers, the elusive viruses and scam artists all sniffing and snooping to steal your data or wreak havoc on your devices. It's a result of these watchful eyes that you can shop online with the comfort of ludicrous credit card information, that your social networks are safe from those unauthorised accesses and the bad viruses do not creep into your computer.

That is the magic: everyone can become a Cyber Avenger. Whether you are bad with code or a socialite master, you have something to do that will be of use to digital city safety. Just like any given city, the roles vary for different types of people. Some Cyber Avengers are clearly very talented. Either they can produce secret ways to write, others discover clues or solve puzzles but a few simply excel in teaching others how to be safe online.

The Cyber Avenger Squad

Permit me, if you please, to introduce our very own Cyber Avenger Squad:

- **Alex:** The Genius of Technology, one who can hack any system. Of course, he hacks for the good of all. He is the one who finds the hidden backdoors which the hackers use and closes them up tight.
- **Maya:** The Investigator with unparalleled panache in unearthing the hidden truth or finding digital traces. She finds the hacker den in less time than it takes to say "password".
- **Sam:** The Coder who can devise codes that even the slyest of viruses can't outsmart. He is somewhat of a digital doctor who will conjure up vaccines to keep your computer healthy.

- **And you!** You're just about to join our league. What will your speciality be? Will you have the code-cracking genius of Alex, the keen investigative skills of Maya or the know-how of a digital doctor la Sam? Maybe you will discover a completely new talent which none of us can even imagine!

The chapters that follow will be our intro to the dangers that were hidden under the digital shadow; they will help us build a fortress around our data and show how to walk on the Internet like a real pro. By the time this book concludes, you will be armed with all the resources to become an ace Cyber Avenger. Now, are you ready to take your first mission?

Cyber Avenger Challenge 1

What are three things you love to do online? What are three things that make you nervous about the Internet?

(Remember, there are no right or wrong answers! Cybersecurity is all about learning and being aware.)

1. _____
2. _____
3. _____

Chapter 2: Know Your Enemy - Cyber Threats 101

Okay, Cyber Avengers! Now that you are up to speed on the dramatic happenings in cyberspace, it is time to meet the bad guys. In an action movie, one has to know who the enemy really is in order to understand how to defeat it. Let's get into the cyber threats and see how we can outsmart them!

Viruses

The Common Cold of the Cyber World!

Have you ever had a cold or the flu? It is just terrible, isn't it? You are so tired, achy and just totally miserable. Your whole system shuts down and all you want to do is go to bed and sleep. Then look on the bright side: computers can get sick too! Their cold is called a virus. Just like a biological virus, spreading from one person to another, creating havoc that is exactly what a computer virus does.

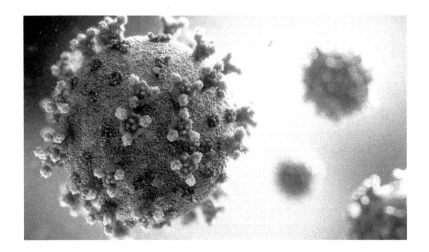

But what is a computer virus? Something like a very tiny, malicious code-a list of instructions to cause damage. Such types of viruses can be found in e-mails that look quite normal, files you download from the Internet or even the websites that you visit. Once they enter your gadget, they are such tiny little devils that create havoc in any system.

Of these, some will invade your computer and make programs crash, important files disappear or even stolen. Whereas some viruses can be only pranks which irritate you, others are serious and can actually cause damage. But do not worry, we will find out how to protect ourselves from those pesky insects later on!

Hackers

Those Sneaky Intruders!

Take for example, the situation in which a person tries to break into your house when you are away. A hacker does pretty much the same job, except this time, the intrusion is on your computer or any other electronic device/equipment. Hackers are those people who break into networks and data illicitly with their technology acumen.

Not all hackers are cut from the same cloth, though. There is the so-called "white hat hacker" who tests cybersecurity companies' defences for weak points. These are more like good guys who might try to break into the bank vault but only in order to show the bank management how it can beef up its security. Those who use such talents for bad things, like stealing money or basically creating havoc, we refer to as "black hat hackers". Those are the ones we need to protect ourselves from.

Phishing

The Bait-and-Switch Trick

Have you ever gone fishing? You put something delicious on the hook to lure in the fish, right? Well, "phishing" is nothing more than a cyber-attack that plays the same trick with you being, well, not the fish but its target in this scam.

Phishing attacks most commonly appear as e-mails, texts or even social media messages but frequently will look like they are from someone you trust. That can include your bank, a company you use or even a friend. Usually, such messages claim that there is some sort of problem with your account, you have won a prize or you need to update information immediately. Otherwise, that click on the link or opening of the attachment may be tantamount to releasing unnecessarily large volumes of personal information to a hacker. Literally, the bait is taken and falls into a trap!

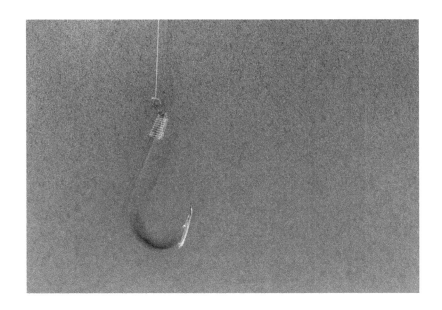

Malware

Another name for Trouble!

Basically, malware is the general term that refers to every form of bad software that damages your gadget. It is one big family, troublemakers included.

- **Viruses:** These little nasties were discussed earlier.
- **Worms:** For example, viruses that can spread on their own and do not need to attach themselves to a file. They are similar to tiny crawlies that can infect an entire network very quickly.
- **Trojans:** These are deceptive in nature, masquerading as harmless programs such as a game or a file you've

downloaded. Yet, once you dare to open them, they release their damaging payload.

- **Ransomware:** It is a form of malware that seizes control of your files, demanding a ransom typically in cryptocurrency in exchange for their release. It's akin to being held hostage, only this time, the confinement is digital.
- **Spyware:** It's like a snitching software that, in secrecy, tracks your activity and swipes information. Like having a spy in one's own computer!

The whole family is a bunch of troublemakers and we have to stay on our toes no matter what!

Cyber Avenger Challenge 2

Unscramble this word to reveal a type of malware that locks up your files and demands payment:

NSORAAERWM

_____

Ask the Expert

QUESTION:

What are the signs that indicate an e-mail might be a phishing scam?

ANSWER:

Good question! Watch out for these red flags:

- **Misspellings and grammatical errors:** Reputable companies usually employ competent editors to avert spelling and grammatical mistakes.
- **Suspicious links:** Mouse over the links, don't click! to see if the address looks strange. Does it match the company's Web site?
- **Urgent or threatening language:** Scammers try to scare you into acting quickly without thinking.

- **Requests for personal information:** No respectable company will be requesting your password or your credit card number by e-mail.

Always consult some trusted adult or go online to check if other people have received the same e-mail and declare it a fraud if in doubt. It always is better being safe than sorry.

Chapter 3: Build Your Digital Fortress using Security Essentials

Now that we've met the enemy, it is time to start building our defences. Think of your digital life like a big old castle: your personal information, accounts and devices are the treasures in your life that you do not want to lose to bandits and thieves. But every castle needs hard walls, strong gates and vigilant guards to help keep the intruders away. In this chapter, we will find out how to build your very own digital fortress!

Passwords

The Keys to Your Kingdom!

Just remember that passwords are the key to all digital kingdoms: e-mail, social networking profiles, online banking and much more. Just like you would never give your home keys to strangers, for the same significant reasons, do not allow your passwords to be taken away without purpose.

Below are a few tips for making ultra-strong passwords:

- **Make it long:** At least make it 12 characters. Think of it as a drawbridge; the longer it is, the harder it is to cross for the enemy!

- **Employ a mixture of characters:** Combine uppercase letters, lowercase letters, numbers and symbols (@, #, $, %, etc.). It's like creating your own secret code that nobody else knows!

- **Don't use personal information:** Avoid using your name, birth date or pet's name. Hackers can easily find it online and may use such information to guess your password.

- **Make it unique:** For God's sake, don't use the same password for every account! That's just like using the same key for your house, car and locker. If the hacker gets one key, he will get into each of them.

- **Use a password manager:** All your passwords are stored in a secure manner with a password manager and all you have to remember is one master password; the password manager will do the rest! It's like an electronic knight in shining armour that guards your keys.

Software Updates

Patch the Holes in Your Armor

Think of a few cracks and holes in your castle walls. The vulnerabilities in the software, including applications and programs that run on your devices are likened to these. These bugs make most hackers jump for joy because they find easy ways to intrude into your system. Luckily, there is one patch for all these updates!

Software updates are significant repairs that patch vulnerabilities, securing yours virtually. They always have new security features, bug fixes and hold the ideal tweaks that keep you guarded against emerging threats. It is, thus absolutely necessary that you go on installing the most recent operating systems - Windows or macOS on your device and update your web browsers such as Chrome or Firefox and other apps on a regular basis. Think of this as reinforcing the walls of your kingdom from an attack by those pesky invaders!

Antivirus Software

Your Digital Guard Dog

An antivirus basically acts as a guard dog for the home. It looks over your devices, protecting them from any potential malware. It is a 24/7 patrol of your files, folder structures and in a nutshell, all the bad, malicious software.

Antivirus software can detect, quarantine and remove it before it will be able to cause damage. It would just about be like having a doctor at your beck and call to find the symptoms of illness, then prescribe medication to cure the same. So, first things first: you install a good antivirus program on your gadgets and update them regularly. Just as one takes his guard dog for its check-up so that he stays in top shape, hail or high water!

Privacy Settings

Manage Your Online Kingdom

You are the king of your online kingdom and you can decide who sees what. Privacy settings include a series of controls usually adopted for managing one's online presence: photos seen by selected people, posted messages and personal information.

Now, stop whatever you're doing and take a moment to review the privacy settings on your social media accounts, online games and other apps. Remember, not everything is meant to be shared with everyone in the wide, wide world. Let your personal information stay personal; know who you're sharing it with. Think about it: It's your castle and the moat stops everyone coming in except those you want to let in!

Cyber Avenger Challenge 3

Now, make a really awesome password for your favourite online game or app using some of the strategies we just discussed. Say it to a trusted adult and see if they can guess it!

_____

Ask the Expert

QUESTION:

What if I forget my passwords?

ANSWER:

Exactly, yes! That is where password managers come in. They will literally help you concoct the most complicated passwords for your various accounts and then remember those for you. But if that does not work for you, then think about a password you shall find easy to memorise yet difficult for other guys to guess. Or think of a phrase meaningful to you but also not containing personally identifiable information. After all, *"ILovePizza4Dinner!"* is infinitely stronger than *"password123"*. But again, if you find yourself in a rough spot, there's always the "Forgot Password" option on most websites and applications.

Chapter 4: Online Safety Adventures

Cyber Avengers, now that your digital castle is being built, it's time to go into the expansive world called the net! But even as you're reaching out for the net with the tightest defences, stay sharp and wary. Keep in mind: this might just be like landing in a new city, where you see great things and have fun while there is also some danger lurking in the alleys. In this chapter, we will discuss the safe and responsible way of traversing a virtual world.

Be More Social Media Smarts

Don't Spill the Beans!

It's a great way to stay in touch with your friends, let the world know what you're thinking and maybe make some new friends from anywhere around the earth. You can go on and post pictures of that amazing vacation you just had or join groups that are in your interests. In fact, it's like virtually partying with the whole world!

But again, it is always best to remember that not all who go online are really who they say they are. Some even try to make fools or take advantage of you. It's sort of like allowing a strange weirdo into your party: you have to watch who you let in.

Think about it: Would you tell your home address to a random person walking on the street?

No way! It's best not to share personal information, like your address, phone number or school name, with people you don't know online. Even with people you do know, it's better to be careful of what you share. If something goes online, taking it off again is very hard to do. Like spilling juice on your favourite shirt, the stain may never come completely off!

Cyberbullying

Stand Up, Speak Out!

There are bullies in the digital world just like in the real world. A simple definition - cyberbullying is the use of technology to harass, threaten, embarrass or target another individual. This torment can take place through social media websites, text messages, e-mails and online video game environments. It is like being followed by a bully, except the unpleasant experience occurs from behind the screen.

It can be in so many forms: somebody posting bad things about you, some mean message or an embarrassing photo of you or frankly, not including you in the online groups. Sometimes it may be hurtful; sometimes it could be scary. But you are not alone.

Should you feel that you are being bullied online, report it to any parent, teacher or counsellor. They may further help in blocking the bully, reporting to the site or higher authorities and getting support for you. This would be just like having a bodyguard away from the bully and someone who stood up for you.

If you see cyberbullying happening to someone else, be an upstander: Speak out and show support. Tell them that you are there for them and advise them to report it to the nearest adult. It's together that we can make the online world a kinder and safer place.

Secure Yourself from Unknowns

Stranger Danger Goes Digital!

You probably do know not to talk to strangers in real life; well, it's just the same rule online. No chatting online with anybody you may not know, no matter how nice the person comes off. You never know who is actually behind that screen. That would kind of be like talking to a stranger with a mask on; you would have absolutely no idea about his intentions.

But don't respond to such online contacts by somebody you don't know. Block and report them on the website or in the app. In other words, slam the door hard in the face of this person. If any stranger asks to meet you in person, let a trusted adult know about it immediately. Remember, at all times your safety is the most important thing.

Ignore Fake News Alerts

Sorting Facts from Fictions

The Internet overflows with information but all of it is not the truth. Fake news includes false or fabricated information spread with an intention to confuse the masses. It can encompass a wide range of subjects from politics and celebrities to health and even the weather. Like a funhouse mirror, it warps reality, making it difficult to discern what is real.

Identifying fake news is the art of being a responsible digital citizen. Following are some helpful tips that can assist in such prospects.

- **Check the source:** Is this information from an established news organisation or is it a website you've never heard of?

Reputable news organisations earn their reputations based on honesty and detailed fact-checking.

- **Find evidence:** Does the article offer supporting proof to what it claims, say quotes from experts or other sources? True news is backed up by evidence.
- **Be sceptical:** Not everything you read online is necessarily true. If something looks too good to be true, most likely it isn't.
- **Do your own research:** Try and gather information from more than one source. Best not to believe in one website or article.

Think of yourself as a detective in the process of putting together details of a crime. You will have to get the entire picture by collecting evidence from everywhere. It's through being critical with information online that you will avoid pitfalls orchestrated by fake news and land on well-informed decisions.

Cyber Avenger Challenge 4

Unscramble this word to reveal a term for false or misleading information spread online: NEKSAEFW

_____

Ask the Expert

QUESTION:

If you have accidentally shared private information online, what would you do?

ANSWER:

Don't panic! First, tell a trusted adult who can help you think through what happened and the steps you can take in order to protect yourself. If your information was on a website or app, you could change the settings to let the public access it as little as possible or even delete the information if it is deletable. You may also report it to that website or app. You may want to change some passwords and monitor your accounts closely for strange activities. It is an act of cleaning, just like cleaning up after the creation of a mess. This might take some time but it is something really important that needs to be done as fast as possible.

Remember, Cyber Avengers, the Internet is this dynamic and exciting place but you have to know some of the dangers it poses and do something to protect yourself. Wise, cautious and responsible. And don't forget you're going to have a lot of fun adventures online!

Chapter 5: Crack the Code of Cybersecurity

Get ready, Cyber Avengers and notch it up! Though we have discussed the very basics of cybersecurity, it is time to dig into the inner details: what tools and techniques professionals use in protecting the digital world. Gear up and be ready to crack some codes, create virtual shields and become a cybersecurity ninja!

Encryption

The Art of Hidden Messages

Have you ever written secret messages to your friend, perhaps in some kind of code that both of you knew? Maybe each letter was replaced by some unique symbol or perhaps shifted down the alphabet. Well, my friend, this is very basically how encryption works!

Encryption is the elaborate process wherein it scrambles information like your messages, e-mails or online purchases so that people gain access only with the right authentication. Think of it as putting your message in a locked box, a safe container to which only the person with the proper key has access. The box remains in plain view but its contents are illegible gibberish to everyone without that key.

Think of it this way, suppose you are writing a card to your friend. If you write your message in plain English, then any person finding the postcard will know what it says. If you write it in some code, then just your friend, who can figure out what the code means, will understand it.

Everything is encrypted on the Internet. It keeps your data away from unwanted prying. Whenever you are typing your credit card number into some site, it's usually encrypted, in most cases, so hackers can't read your data when it travels on the web. Even messages and e-mails can be encrypted, keeping all those conversations private from people who maybe snooping around.

Firewalls

The Digital Drawbridge!

Remember that castle in Chapter 3? Think of a firewall like a digital drawbridge that watches and controls who gets through and by which route. At the very basic level, a network is a collection of devices connected to something, e.g., your computer, phone or smart TV. Firewalls sit between your network and the rest of the Internet to watch all the traffic coming into and out of your device.

Just think about the security guard at the entrance to a castle, checking the ID of any person who is willing to get in. The only difference is that the firewall checks every bit of data: every e-mail, every request to load a certain web page and any file that is downloaded against a set of rules. If the data has passed those sets of rules, then it allows the data to pass through. If it doesn't comply, the firewall prevents access, much like a drawbridge lifted to keep out uninvited guests.

Two-Factor Authentication (2FA)

Double the Security!

Ever had to enter some type of code that was sent to your phone right after you were trying to log into an account? This process is called two-factor authentication, 2FA or sometimes multi-factor authentication as well. It's having two locks on your door; even if someone somehow picks one lock, they still can't get inside your house without the second key.

How 2FA works: One logs in like they normally would, entering their username and password but then enters in a second form of verification something like a code that was mailed by phone or e-mail. That second code proves it's really you trying to get into the account and not just some person who happened to guess your password right.

So, 2FA adds another layer of security to your online accounts, making it super difficult for any hacker to access them. Even if the hacker succeeds in stealing your password, he still cannot gain access to your account without the second code.

Backup Your Treasure

Don't Put All Your Eggs in One Basket!

Just imagine all of your favourite toys in one box and then that particular box gets lost or breaks into pieces; that is a disaster. Ironically, the same can be believed to happen to your data: just one accident at your computer, your phone stolen, malware hijacks your files; and one day they can make you lose everything, your favourite pictures, school projects, music and many more.

That is exactly the reason why periodic backups of data are of utmost importance. It means making copies of your important files and storing them somewhere else,

which is almost like having a spare key for your house; if you lose your original key, at least you know you have another one, which will get you in.

The data can be backed up in a few ways:

- **External hard drive:** A portable storage device that you can plug into your computer.
- **Cloud storage:** This is an online service whereby data is maintained on remote servers. Some of the best cloud storages include Google Drive, Dropbox and iCloud.
- **USB stick:** This is a very small, portable storage device that you can plug into any computer.

You safeguard yourself from such sudden incidents and also make sure that your digital treasures do not end up getting lost.

Cyber Avenger Challenge 5

Enable two-factor authentication on at least one of your online accounts. You may need to ask a parent or guardian to help you with this.

Ask the Expert

QUESTION:

Is the encryption fool-proof?

ANSWER:

Though encryption gives the maximum possible protection to data, it is never unbreakable. Since any lock can be picked with enough knowledge and patience, so too can encryption be broken. But, of course, that is easier said than done! In the case of good encryption, a hacker will have to invest a lot of time and consume many resources to finally break it. Because of this, it is important to talk about other security functions that may further support passwords for instance, 2FA and encryption. All these create many layers of security that will make it difficult for hackers to steal data quite hard.

Chapter 6: The Future with Emerging Tech and Cybersecurity

So, put your Cyber Avenger helmets on and hold on to something as we blast this final frontier of technology. The domain of technology continues to grow, making new vistas that are getting really exciting toward cybersecurity. This chapter examines just a few of these important, game-changing technologies that will likely define the future of cybersecurity and how you can jump into this engaging field.

Artificial Intelligence (AI) in Cybersecurity

Robots to the Rescue!

Do you remember watching movies or perhaps series that include robots helping a detective track down the criminals? Well, in this world of cybersecurity, such machines are already working their fingers to the bone! Artificial intelligence, more commonly referred to as AI is a type of technology that helps machines learn and make decisions much like human beings. In cybersecurity, AI has been employed in identifying and responding to threats with an efficiency and speed not previously conceivable.

Think of AI as the brilliant sidekick to cybersecurity experts, one that looks through tons of data for patterns or anomalies that may presage a cyberattack. Consider, for a moment, the difficulty of finding the needle in the haystack: the work of a human analyst-say, a few million lines of code combed through, line by line, in search of a single vulnerability. But what AI can do is get it done fast and with accuracy like a super-powered magnet finding the needle in seconds.

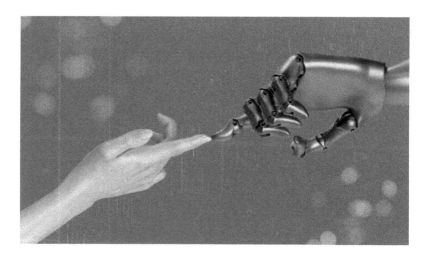

AI can certainly undertake the automation of such tasks as scanning for malware or phishing e-mails and allow human effort to focus on more complicated issues. An army of tireless robots is elbowing day and night in relentless battle, protecting your computer from all sorts of dangers.

The Internet of Things (IoT)

Is your Smart Fridge Online?

Have you ever heard of this thing called the Internet of Things or IoT for short? It is basically a network of all those very well-known devices, starting from your fridge and thermostat to your toothbrush, all on the Internet. They all collect the required data, talk to each other and may even be remotely controlled. It is somewhat like having a conversation with your fridge so that it might prepare a shopping list on its own or let you know when you're out of milk.

But then, with all that connectivity, it opens a whole new world of cybersecurity risks. Imagine a hacker taking control of your thermostat or turning off your lights. Or, even more eerily, your smart fridge shares a list of the food you buy with some marketing company. Almost like some strange man overhearing your conversations or following you around your home.

The IoT is very convenient but it's so nice to understand the security vulnerabilities and take steps in protecting your smart devices, just like you would do with your computer or phone. This would mean using a strong password, keeping software current and being aware of the information you give these devices.

Ethical Hacking

The "Robin Hoods" of the Digital World

We talked about the practice of hacking in Chapter 2 but let's recognise that all hackers don't wear a black hat. Ethical hackers also known as "white hat hackers" use their skills to help companies and other organisations improve their computer security. In many ways, they are like the Robin Hoods of the computer world, using their powers for good. Remember Alex, the Genius of Technology from our Cyber Avenger squad?

Unlike unethical hackers who take advantage of weaknesses for their benefit, ethical hackers utilise their skills to find and fix security weaknesses. Organisations hire them to try and break into their systems in the very way as would their maliciously minded counterparts. Only rather than causing damage, they present their findings to the organisation with the aim that it may fix the gaps and secure its security.

That is a very challenging and rewarding career as well as being in a position to use such technical skills in trying to make a difference. You are protecting not just computers and data but you are helping to keep people and businesses safe from cyberattacks.

The Importance of Staying Informed

Cybersecurity is always Changing!

Technology is fast-moving and it is no different when talking about security for technological systems. Every day, new threats appear; even worse, hackers seem to always find ways to breach the latest barriers and rules. That's why staying up to date with all the happenings in the cybersecurity world is a real must.

It's like learning new steps in dancing; one has to practice all the time and learn new steps in order to be ahead. In this regard, knowing what is current out there will assist you in knowing how to protect yourself and your data.

There are several ways through which cybersecurity can be updated:

- **Stay current with cybersecurity news:** Follow reputable cybersecurity websites and blogs that report on the latest threats and trends.

- **Listen to podcasts:** Many interesting podcasts focus on cybersecurity topics and can be an engaging and informative resource for such learning.

- **Watch videos:** There is a lot one could learn about cybersecurity from YouTube tutorials, explanations and even live hacking demonstrations.

- **Attend conferences and workshops:** Attend any locally available or even online events to learn from experts in the field and network with fellow cybersecurity enthusiasts.

- **Follow cybersecurity experts on social media:** Most of the cybersecurity professionals share their tips and other inside information on Twitter and LinkedIn.

In fact, it provides you with the real meaning of a good digital citizen wherein you are protecting yourself and others from cyber threats. After all, knowledge is power!

Cyber Avenger Challenge 6

Research one of the following emerging technologies discussed in this chapter (AI, IoT or ethical hacking). Write a short report on it, including its potential benefits and risks. How might it be leveraged to better cybersecurity?

_____

_____

_____

_____

_____

_____

_____

_____

_____

_____

_____

_____

_____

_____

_____

_____

_____

Ask the Expert

QUESTION:

Could you keep me posted on the latest developments in cyber security?

ANSWER:

There are a lot of ways to remain involved in cybersecurity. Here are a few ideas as we discussed earlier:

- **Read cybersecurity news!**
- **Listen to podcasts related to Cyber Security!**
- **Watch videos from Cyber Security technologists!**
- **Attend conferences and workshops!**
- **Follow cybersecurity experts on social media!**

The mere fact of being aware will update one as a better digital citizen and protect oneself along with others from cyber threats.

Chapter 7: Become a Cyber Hero

Cyber Avengers, you have traversed so much distance! You learned to identify the lurking threats in the cyber platform, build a fortress around your information and surf cautiously. This is not the end of this journey though. In fact, just the beginning! The Internet is never at rest and whenever there is a change in motion, associated risks are forever there too. Well, sure enough, from now on, you are equipped with all the knowledge and skills to keep one step ahead of the bad guys.

It is within this final chapter that we enter the exciting field of cybersecurity careers and point out resources for the young, aspiring cyberist to be, then finally take that last mission application of your new skills learned.

Careers in Cybersecurity

Protecting the Digital World!

Many people do not even realise that this world exists: an entire universe of professions serving to protect the digital universe. There is much demand for cybersecurity professionals and there are numerous options for those interested in entering the field. It's like being a superhero but instead of fighting super-powered bad guys, you use your technical powers to protect people and businesses from cyber threats.

Just a few examples of what's in store in the line of exciting careers in cybersecurity:

Ethical Hacker

An ethical hacker is also known as a white-hat hacker or a penetration tester. He is an expert in computer security using methods like those of hackers which lead to discovering system, network and application vulnerabilities like our Alex from Cyber Avenger squad; unlike evil hackers, though, he is "the good guy". In fact, an organisation can purposefully hire an ethical hacker to lawfully and ethically attack its systems to surface the weaknesses that may be exploited by cyber-crooks. The basic intent of their goals is to find these weaknesses and patch them before actual hackers get the opportunity to exploit them.

By nature, every cybersecurity expert needs to wear the hat of a cyber thief to predict the possible direction of an attack. For that purpose, they will need to test the system for vulnerabilities in search of unpatched software, poor passwords, firewalls or unsecured channels of communication. When found, they report them to the company with their recommendations for fixing those problems. Besides what was mentioned above, ethical hackers also conduct social engineering tests such as they artfully deceive employees into disclosing sensitive information like passwords through phishing emails or other types of fraud.

An ethical hacker requires knowledge about a variety of programming languages, network protocols and operating systems. Other tools and utilities include *Metasploit*, *Wireshark* and *Burp Suite* that a reformed hacker uses to conduct effective cyber-attacks. Creativity and technical skill are called for here in equal measure; after all, sometimes a tester will want to think outside of the box to find a way that nobody knows how to crack a secure system. Ethical hackers help organisations comply with regulations such as GDPR, HIPAA among others, demanding the highest degrees of care for the protection of data.

Security Analyst

The Security Analyst is literally the front line of defence for organisations wanting to protect themselves against the growing menace of cyber threats. Their responsibilities majorly include keen monitoring of an organisation's networks on the lookout for any suspicious or unauthorised activity. By employing specialised software tools, they examine security logs, identify vulnerabilities and set off brakes to avoid a potential breach. In proactive terms, Security Analysts pursue threats and weaknesses in attempts to neutralise them before actual damage can be caused.

They are the first lines of defence when there is an incident involving malware attacks or data breaches. They conduct research into the issue, go about containing the threat and deploy fixes to mitigate the damage. After they contain the incident, they provide a report regarding the attack and recommend measures that need to be taken by an organisation to prevent similar incidents in the near future. Apart from this, security analysts are heavily engaged in outlining the security policies that ensure that an organisation follows the relevant cybersecurity policies.

Success in this position calls for a keenly attentive and well-informed security analyst with current cyber threats such as *ransomware* and *phishing*. Analysts should constantly increase their knowledge and develop their skills because the threats posed by cybercriminals do not stop evolving. It is an excellent job for any person who has sharp analytical acumen, pays attention to fine details and maintains their calm under pressure.

Security Engineer

A security engineer will have an important role in the design, implementation and upkeep of the technical defence that is placed to guard the digital infrastructure of an organisation. They are architects of systems that prevent unauthorised access to data and other cyberattacks. They develop firewalls, intrusion detection systems and encryption protocols among other means, hand in hand, working together to keep sensitive information safe. Do you remember Sam, the member of the fantastic Cyber Avenger squad we talked about in Chapter 1?

They develop and improve the security presently available. They analyse vulnerabilities and do penetration testing which enables them to show weaknesses in the systems they have worked so hard to build. If a hole is exposed, they rush to patch it and ensure that the defences of the organisation stay up to date. They will be responsible for imparting knowledge to their other IT colleagues in the ways of getting effective security properly implemented within an organisation. Security engineering calls for great knowledge in computer networks, programming and system architecture. Such an engineer must have knowledge about *VPNs, firewalls* and *methods of encryption* to devise efficient security solutions. Since the threats change day by day, security engineers are expected to be more innovative, adaptive and one step ahead of any would-be intruder.

Cyber Forensic Investigator

The Cyber Forensic Investigator develops this complex science of investigating digital crimes. Similar to a detective in the physical world, their work can range from merely collecting evidence to a detailed analysis of computers, mobile phones and networks. Just like Maya from our Cyber Avenger Squad, they have an important job of finding how a breach occurred, who did it and preserving digital evidence which may come out to be vital in court cases.

Whether it be an attack through a data breach, insider threat or malware, forensic investigators piece together a puzzle as to what happened and how in the future.

Cyber forensic investigators work for both law enforcement agencies and corporate legal departments. They're supposed to present hard evidence that should be admissible and stand in court. They are expected to recover deleted files, track user activity, decrypt encrypted data through the use of advanced tools and document their findings carefully for later use in courts. Their work can range from so complex with matters dealing with corporate espionage to tracking down ransomware attacks that target multimillion-dollar ransoms.

Broad knowledge of digital forensic tools such as *EnCase* or *FTK*, Forensic Toolkit and legal requirements with respect to the possession of digital evidence is what would be needed. Basically, broad experiences in networking, system administration and encryption are better. It would therefore be a career that will be equally challenging and rewarding, promising special attention to detail, acuteness of problems being solved and doing all this under pressure.

Malware Analyst

A malware analyst's job is to look at malicious software and figure out how it works. They will be studying viruses, worms, Trojans and other malware to learn how they infect systems, spread themselves and damage data. Analysts employ reverse engineering to investigate the attack's source, method of operation and the destruction that can potentially be caused in looking at the code behind the attack. This information is really crucial in coming up with patches and defence mechanisms against future harm.

Malware analysts frequently find themselves in a laboratory setting, where they can safely execute and observe the behaviours of various malware. Employing sandbox environments and disassemblers, they meticulously examine the code line by line, pinpointing the commands it executes and the techniques it employs to evade detection. The insights they gather contribute to the development of updates for antivirus software and serve to inform fellow cybersecurity professionals on how to recognise and thwart potential future malware attacks.

A malware analyst should have in-depth knowledge of programming languages such as *C++, Python* and *Assembly*; hands-on experience with operating systems and network protocols is also a must. The position calls for very solid knowledge and an analytical approach, all in a methodical stance towards problem-solving, considering that it deals with very minute details about the operation of software with hardware.

Penetration Tester

They are professionally identified as pen testers and work to identify infrastructural weaknesses in the organisation, allowing the emulation of real cyber-attacks. The objective is to test how strong the security systems are by looking for the weaknesses that one would use if they were a bad hacker. To gain unauthorised access, the penetration tester would apply any techniques from the popular arsenal such as exploiting outdated software or weak passwords.

They will be reporting their results to the company with recommendations on security improvement.

In penetration testing, attacks against web applications, networks and internal systems are at times thoroughly planned and executed. A pen tester needs to think like a hacker by using innovative ideas and ways of uncovering undercover weaknesses. They ensure that whenever an attack would happen, the security of the organisation will not be dumped. Not only that, pen testers also ensures that an organisation may be able to abide by cybersecurity regulations through regular audits and testing procedures from ground compliance to standard regulations.

This requires good knowledge of networking, coding and security protocols. Knowledge of *Nmap, Kali Linux* and *Metasploit* are vital tools in the execution of tests. In addition to technical skills, a penetration tester must possess good communication skills because very often this specialist has to explain quite complex security questions to business persons who are not technically oriented.

Security Consultant

A Security Consultant is an advisor who helps different organisations improve their cybersecurity. In contrast to either the security analyst or security engineer which are parts of an organisation, the consultant works with many clients and advises on how to protect digital assets. The consultant will assess the current security posture of an organisation, identify vulnerabilities and provide recommendations for improving security.

Another group of security consultants has tailored solutions, whether it is in implementing new security technologies or in creating policies that would deal with the threats posed by the latter. Most of the time, consultants are hired as experts after a breach or security incident has occurred to prevent further attacks. This is also legally helpful in satisfying compliance regulations and regulatory requirements of data protection for an organisation. Since cybersecurity is so dynamic arena, the Security Consultant will always continually update their knowledge on new threats and trends so they then can advise their client on how to be proactive.

Against such a background, practice success in security consultancy calls for adequate grasp of cybersecurity concepts in addition to strong analytical skills that include the capacity to present complex technical information in forms that non-technical people can access. Consultants, more often than not have CISSP *(Certified Information Systems Security Professional)* or CISM *(Certified Information Security Manager)* certification to back up their knowledge.

Incident Responder

An Incident Responder is a security professional called to action in the case an organisation has been exposed to a cyberattack. They are like a first line of defence against a cyber-breach where their critical responsibility is to cut the losses, determine the root cause and reinstate the affected systems. Incident responders work according to a given process to contain, eradicate and recover from threats to bring back lost data or services. They then carry out extensive post-incident analysis to prevent attacks in the future and improve the organisation's security position.

Incident responders are those who have to think on their feet and act correctly under immense stress since the speed of reactions directly correlates with how far a cyber-attack may spread. They work extensively with other IT and cybersecurity teams, bringing cohesion to their response. Once an immediate crisis has been resolved, incident responders write comprehensive reports detailing how the breach occurred, how they handled it and what should be done to keep it from happening again. This entails understanding both the level of the network security status and expertise within malware analysis and forensic investigation, alongside responsiveness to different forms of cyber-attacks like *DDoS* and *ransomware* attacks. Most importantly, the individual needs to have good communication skills since an incident responder is supposed to relay technical findings to non-technical executives and stakeholders.

Keep in mind that this is just the tip of the iceberg! In cybersecurity, there are numerous professions which all come with different challenges and various types of thrills. More importantly, you can dive into a career that best fits your interests and skills. If you enjoy solving puzzles, you will want to be a forensic investigator. In case you usually think creatively, then you'll find your job enjoyable if you are appointed as a security engineer. And if you like teaching, you may be interested in being a cybersecurity educator.

Developing Your Skills

Becoming a Cyber Pro!

Ready for an upgrade in cybersecurity skills? Well, the young aspiring cyber enthusiasts have these resources at their beck and call. Actually, this is like having a whole library on cybersecurity.

A few starting points follow:

Coding Classes

One major step that you can take towards your path to cybersecurity is learning to code. It will help you understand the functioning of software and systems, their weak points and at best, how you can come up with your own security utility. You may not be an expert coder to land in the industry, but a grasp of programming languages definitely sets you apart from the competition.

You will actually start by learning *Python* and *JavaScript* because both are very relevant in cybersecurity. It is quite easy to get into Python, which is very popular; it is put to use from scripting to automate security functions to malware analysis. Meanwhile, *HTML* and *CSS* will show you how websites work technically. It is also very important for *SQL* to handle a database and actually act as a gatekeeper against injection-type attacks. Later in the learning path, advanced lower-level languages of *C* and *C++* will be provided for you to review some of the deep interactions such as how malware interfaces with hardware.

The classes start with very basic lessons in coding and can advance to more advanced skill lessons. *Codecademy, Scratch* and *FreeCodeCamp* are the main websites that lead a good starting point for the beginners. To advance your skills, cybersecurity coding courses on Udemy and Coursera go above and beyond the basics, knowing how to create your own security tools or testing against systems to look for security issues.

Online Courses and Tutorials

The best ways to acquire knowledge about cybersecurity are likely through online classes and tutorials. You will be able to learn everything from the basic level of cybersecurity all the way through to the advanced levels of penetration testing and ethical hacking on highly reputable platforms. With these, you can learn at your own pace because they provide courses that are developed by field professionals, so you get quality and updated information.

Among the well-liked options to consider are *Coursera, Udemy, edX* and *Khan Academy.* Many of these websites introduce a wide variety of courses in every important cybersecurity topic imaginable from network security and cryptography to ethical hacking and incident response. Moreover, *Coursera* and *edX* offer content from top-ranked universities in the world with much fuller classes and at times, certifications that will also look good on your resume. Additionally, there's a wealth of free cybersecurity tutorials and walkthroughs on YouTube, made by experts; this makes it an excellent supplementary resource.

With that said, if you want to get more practical practice, then I suggest you carry on with *TryHackMe* or *Hack The Box* because both of these have labs and emulations of real situations where you could go ahead and test your hacking and defence skills. Both provide hands-on exposure of realistic cyber-attacks and their problems for problem solving in a contained environment.

Cybersecurity Competitions

Another fun and learning way, full of vigour is participation in cybersecurity competitions. The most known form is Capture the Flag *(CTF)* event, whereby one solves puzzles or tries to gain access or take advantage of vulnerabilities in systems. CTFs are definitely a good way to apply knowledge, sharpen up experience under pressure but most importantly, they help build in students a sense of cooperation by friendly competition with other peers.

Most of them are based on a set of challenges: reverse engineering, web security, cryptography and forensics. So, you can taste a little bit of everything. Events are really common on platforms like CTFTime, PicoCTF and OverTheWire; they have entries for beginners and pros. Many universities and cybersecurity societies organise CTFs every year, giving really good opportunities to test your skills against other peers around the world.

All of that doing well or even just participating in such competitions clearly beefs up your resume for potential employers. Most of the CTFs are maintained and performed by famous tech companies themselves whereby one can show their skills to recruiters in search of fresh talent. The environment, with two great poles of competitiveness and collaboration within, helps one learn from peers and mentors as one comes together to work on complex challenges.

Mentorship Programs

Learning from Industry Experts, just about the best way to fast-track your career is through knowledge from an industry pro: Mentorship programs will offer you an experienced expert in cybersecurity to give direction, counsel and insider insight. You could receive career advice, as well as feedback on decisions you're making, while mentors will even share personal experiences regarding real-world cyber challenges.

In the same breath, mentoring in the cybersecurity field such as *CyberPatriot* and *Girls Who Code* opens up an opportunity for young students to connect with experiences from the field. You learn from that mentor relationship things that are not going to come from textbooks or online classes: how to stay current, advice on certification or career paths, even job placement assistance. A good mentor will also provide you with specific feedback regarding your work and may even challenge you to initiate new projects that you might not have considered.

So many times, mentorship relationships produce lifelong professional contacts; your mentor can become a critical part of your professional network. Having a mentor means you are not walking this path alone if and when you encounter a difficult technical situation or are questioning which career path to take.

Cybersecurity Certifications

Certifications remain a good way of proving your skills and letting the world of potential employers know whether you do have whatever they need for a cybersecurity job. They can range from entry to expert levels and many times these things become requirements upon employment. Among the entry-level, most recognised is CompTIA Security+ dealing with basic elements of network security, threat management among many others. It does serve as an excellent starting point for people just beginning their careers in cybersecurity.

Later, one should move on to middle and specialised certifications like Certified Ethical Hacker, Certified Information Systems Security Professional or Certified Information Security Manager. All these different certifications reflect specialisations in one aspect: ethical hacking, risk management and information security respectively. Other certifications include the Global Information Assurance Certification which offers a suite of exams in focused topics such as penetration testing, incident response and forensic analysis.

These certifications can be obtained only after great study and the ability to pass an exam. However, once again, it really pays off. Not only will you be able to obtain certification in a lot of cybersecurity topics, but you will also be more marketable for jobs and most likely be seeking higher-level security analysis, engineering or consulting jobs.

Internships and Hands-On Experience

The Best Teacher While knowledge in books, courses and competitions is important, nothing says the process of learning cybersecurity is valid until it's hands-on. An internship also provides you with the prospect of harnessing your skills in a professional setting. You can find cybersecurity related internships within tech companies, government agencies and even non-governmental organisations; these expose you to tasks where you actually work on projects, help in defence against cyber-attacks or enforce security protocols.

Many of these internships will also offer plenty of definitions regarding what in cybersecurity floats your boat. Maybe it's ethical hacking, incident response or security consulting. They will not only provide you with valuable hands-on experience but also help you to lay a professional network that could give rise to job offers upon graduation. If it is not possible soon, then you may consider creating your own cybersecurity projects. You can set up a home lab using *VirtualBox* or *Kali Linux* to practice penetration testing, malware analysis or network security. Most working cybersecurity professionals do personal projects that they can later show in their portfolios and during interviews to prove skills and commitment to a prospective employer.

Cyber Avenger Squad Final Mission

Now that you have learned so much about cybersecurity, it's time to actually share your knowledge. Your final challenge is to indeed create a cybersecurity awareness campaign in your school and community. Time to be that cyber superhero and actually make a difference in the lives of the people around you.

Mission Objective: Design a cybersecurity awareness campaign that will help inform and empower your school or community to be safe online.

Mission Details

- **Identify your audience:** Whom do you want to reach? Classmates, younger students, parents, teachers and the community - all of these? Develop a message that will catch their needs and interest.

- **Choose your message:** What are some major tips in cybersecurity that you want to be portrayed? Focus on the most critical and relevant to your audience.

- **Create your materials:** Get creative! Design posters, flyers, social media posts or maybe a small video to spread around your message. Make them catchy with visuals and tone while keeping language simple. Add a call to action that encourages people to take action and improve their cybersecurity.

- **Share your campaign:** Get permission to put up your documents around your school, in your community or post them online to share with friends and family. Use social media to spread the word via e-mail or other platforms to get the message across to as many as possible.

Remember, Cyber Avengers, a safer digital world is a constant struggle! The word is out for us all to become more aware, informed and protect ourselves and others from the cyber dangers out there. Keep learning, keep investigating and may your powers be used for good!

Cyber Avenger Pledge

I, *[Your Name],* hereby pledge to undertake solemnly to be a worthy digital citizen.

- I will protect my personal information and not share it with strangers online.
- I will create strong passwords and keep them confidential.
- I will be kind and respectful to others online.
- I will not engage in cyberbullying or any other harmful online behaviour.
- I will report any suspicious activity or cyber threats to a trusted adult immediately.
- I will continue to learn about cybersecurity and use my knowledge to help others stay safe online.

By signing this pledge, I commit to using my powers for good and making the Internet a safer place for everyone.

Signed,
[Your Signature]

Date: *[Date]*

Cyber Avengers Glossary

- **Antivirus Software:** A program that protects computers from viruses and malware.
- **Cyberbullying:** A use of technology to threaten, frighten or embarrass someone.
- **Cybersecurity:** The practice of protecting computers, networks and data from unauthorised access, theft or misuse.
- **Data:** Information stored on a computer or online.
- **Hacker:** A person who uses their computer skills to access someone's systems or data without authorisation.
- **Malware:** A harmful software like viruses, worms and Trojans.
- **Password:** A secret word or phrase used to access a computer, an account or a device.
- **Phishing:** The art of scamming where attackers try to trick you into giving them your personal information.
- **Privacy Settings:** Settings to control who can see your information through your profile online.
- **Social media:** Websites and applications allowing people to connect with friends and share information online.
- **Software Update:** A patch or an improvement made to a computer program or an application.
- **Virus:** A type of malware that can replicate itself and spread to other machines.

Closing Note for the Cyber Avengers

Congratulations, Cyber Avengers!

By now, you should be educated and can start your journey in cyberspace. With great power comes great responsibility. Continue to use deeper knowledge wisely and be inquisitive. Continue to look around for new ways of protecting not just yourself but also others in cyberspace.

The future of cybersecurity is in your hands!

Notes

About the Author

Jignesh carries over 11 years of experience in the line of cybersecurity. He's worked with different consulting firms even some of the big ones of the Big 4 helping literally tons of clients to make their cybersecurity robust over these years. So, he knows a bit too much about everything with regards to cybersecurity and people look at him like the go-to expert.

This is the reason why, motivated with a passion to protect the digital world and being concerned for the future generation, he decided to pen it down. His first publication - *A Beginner's Compass to Navigating Cyber Security* is dedicated to the commitment in guiding and educating young minds who are willing to venture into this world. This will greatly benefit teenagers particularly those between the age of 13 and 25 years who become very interested in technology and embrace most elements of learning about cybersecurity.

I mean, Jignesh was there too, those few rough spots when young people were trying to figure out how to get into cybersecurity during his career. Thankful for it, he is all in and pays it forward with the mentorship and coaching of aspiring cybersecurity pros by sharing knowledge to help them figure it out.

When he is not working or writing, he spends quality time with his awesome wife, Varsha and considers the bond he shares with her as one of the core elements of family and friendship. His educational zeal and fervour for cybersecurity inspire many to this date and he enjoys continuing to give back to the community.